What's in this book

This book belongs to

_____

我们一起玩 Let's all play

学习内容 Contents

沟通 Communication

称呼家庭成员
Address family members

生词 New words

★ 爸爸　father, dad
★ 妈妈　mother, mum
★ 姐姐　elder sister
★ 弟弟　younger brother
★ 狗　　dog
　和　　and
　一起　together
　玩　　to play

句式 Sentence patterns

姐姐和弟弟一起玩。
The elder sister and the younger brother play together.

跨学科学习 Project

制作家谱，介绍家庭成员
Make a family tree and describe your family members

文化 Cultures

中国家庭亲属称谓
Chinese kinship terms

Get ready

1 Do you have any pets?

2 What is your favourite family activity?

3 What is Hao Hao's family going to play?

bà ba
爸爸

爸爸和我们一起玩。

jiě jie
姐姐

姐姐和我一起玩。

弟弟和我一起玩。

妈妈快来，到你了。

谢谢妈妈！

狗
gǒu

小狗和我们一起玩。

Let's think

1 Recall the story and number the pictures in order. Write in Chinese.

四

2 Recall the story and look at the pictures. Put a tick or a cross.

New words

1 Learn the new words.

狗

姐姐

弟弟

和

妈妈

爸爸

一起 玩

2 Draw lines to match the words to the pictures.

爸爸　　弟弟　　姐姐　　狗　　妈妈

🎧 **03** **1** Look, listen and match.

🎧 **04** **2** Look at the pictures. Listen to the sto

d say.

3 Write the letters. Role-play with your friend.

a

b

c

d

1 ☐ 和小狗一起玩。

2 姐姐和 ☐ 一起玩。

3 我和弟弟一起玩。

☐

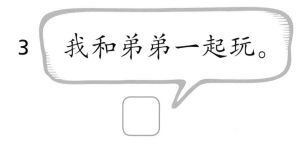

Task

Respond to the questions your friend asks. Draw a picture of your family.

你有姐姐/弟弟吗？

她/他叫什么名字？

她/他几岁？

Game

Who are they going to meet? Listen to your teacher and draw the paths.

Song

🎧 **05** Listen and sing.

我的家，

我的家，

有爸爸和妈妈，

有姐姐和弟弟，

还有小狗布朗尼。

课堂用语 Classroom language

非常好。

Excellent.

排队。

Queue up.

围圆圈。

Form a circle.

写一写 Write

1 Learn and trace the stroke.

撇点

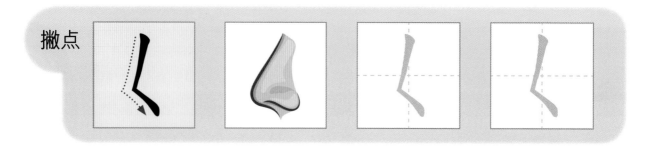

2 Learn the component. Trace 女 to complete the characters.

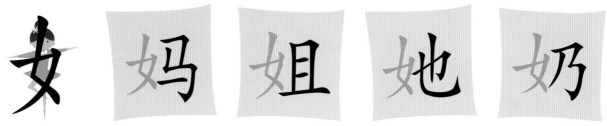

女 妈 姐 她 奶

3 Find the flowers with 女 inside. Colour them red and the others yellow.

4 Trace and write the character.

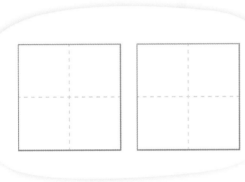

5 Write and say.

汉字小常识 Did you know?

Many components provide clues to how a character sounds.

Can you guess the pronunciation of the characters?

mǎ
马 妈 吗 码 骂

Cultures

1 Look at the Chinese family tree. Circle the elder sister and the younger brother.

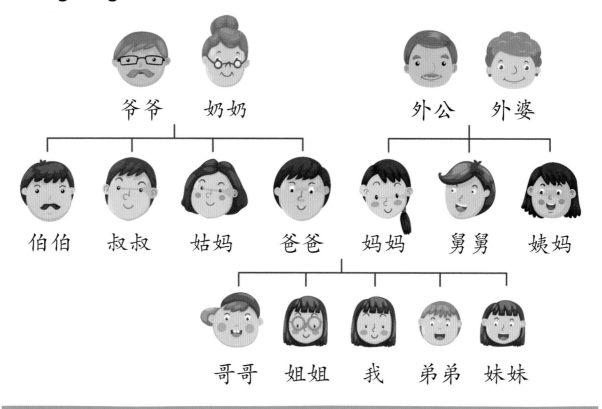

Different kinship terms are used to show whether a family member is younger or older, or whether this person is on the father's side or mother's side.

2 Do you have these relatives? Circle the leaves if you do.

Mother's side			Father's side	
舅舅 mother's brother		uncle	father's elder brother	伯伯
			father's younger brother	叔叔
姨妈 mother's sister		aunt	father's sister	姑妈

Project

1 Make your family tree.

2 Show the family tree to your friend. Talk about your family.

我叫＿＿＿＿，我＿＿岁。

我爸爸叫＿＿＿。

我妈妈叫＿＿＿。

我姐姐叫＿＿＿，她＿＿岁。

我弟弟叫＿＿＿，他＿＿岁。

温习 Checkpoint

1 Play with your friend. Choose a colour and complete the tasks on card A and card B in each round.

A **1**
Say 'thank you' in Chinese.
∀

A **3**
姐姐和弟弟一起玩。
∀

A **2**
我叫玲玲。
∀

A **3**
姐姐六岁。
∀

B **3**
What is the meaning?
B

B **3**
What is the question for A? Say in Chinese.
B

B **1**
Reply in Chinese.
B

B **1**
Say the rest of the numbers up to ten.

When you complete a task, you will get the mark(s) on the card.

A

1

一　三　五
七　九

A

B

2

What is the question for A? Say in Chinese.

B

2 Work with your friend. Colour the stars and the chillies.

Words and sentences	说	读	写
爸爸	☆	☆	🌶
妈妈	☆	☆	☆
姐姐	☆	☆	🌶
弟弟	☆	☆	🌶
狗	☆	☆	🌶
和	☆	🌶	🌶
一起	☆	🌶	🌶
玩	☆	🌶	🌶
姐姐和弟弟一起玩。	☆	🌶	🌶

Address family members	☆

3 What does your teacher say?

My teacher says …

分享 Sharing

Words I remember

爸爸	bà ba	father, dad
妈妈	mā ma	mother, mum
姐姐	jiě jie	elder sister
弟弟	dì di	younger brother
狗	gǒu	dog
和	hé	and

| 一起 | yī qǐ | together |
| 玩 | wán | to play |

Other words

| 我们 | wǒ men | we, us |
| 小 | xiǎo | small |

Oxford University Press is a department of the University of Oxford.
It furthers the University's objective of excellence in research, scholarship,
and education by publishing worldwide. Oxford is a registered trade mark of
Oxford University Press in the UK and in certain other countries

Published in Hong Kong by
Oxford University Press (China) Limited
39th Floor, One Kowloon, 1 Wang Yuen Street, Kowloon Bay,
Hong Kong

Illustrated by Anne Lee and Wildman

Photographs for reproduction permitted by Dreamstime.com

China National Publications Import & Export (Group) Corporation is an authorized distributor of
Oxford Elementary Chinese.

Please contact content@cnpiec.com.cn or 86-10-65856782

ISBN: 978-0-19-082139-5

10 9 8 7 6 5 4